A TEENAGER'S MEMOIR

A BOOK CONSISTING OF COLLECTION OF POEMS WHICH MAKES AN EFFORT TO MOVE YOUR HEART AND SOUL.

SHREYASH S JAISWAL

To Mom and Dad,

You now know that I do write poetries and you have also read some of them. I have learnt everything that I know, from you. Wish I could be a person who comes anywhere near your expectations.

Contents

Contents

Contents

Preface

All this began with a challenge and this book is just a try to replicate how much I have learned till today. This book started to take shape almost seven years ago from the date of publishing and as it says, it is a 'memoir'. A memoir is an account of one's personal life and experiences. A teenager's mind is like a color palate that is used to paint a beautiful picture, the only catch is that the picture which is painted is often overlooked. All the chaos is the reason that brings order to one's life.

This book, not only records the memories but the journey of my poetries that made me what I am today. All those complex sentences were a few silly words down the line when I first started. The book is my reflection on the understanding of poetry.

Never have I pressured myself to write or to make sense when I write. Poetry is like a flowing river, the depth of it is in understanding it. Each of the poems in this book has its own stand towards the perspective that I have of things in my mind.

A reader's mind is often too intricate or fragile to grasp the things that are written between the lines. The book offers you the journey, from a few silly words making sense to phrases that are even beyond my comprehension. Take a seat and hold the book however you like to and give it a read.

Acknowledgements

I often try to acknowledge myself.

1. One Motivation

I was curious to write
And was furious to be bright
I was jealous of my friend
Who was best from top to end.

*

I was stuck in the middle
As was not fit as a fiddle
I was in a lot of pain
And wanted to get up once again

*

I wanted to start from the first
And wanted to quench my thirst
I did it till the end
And met that old friend

*

His jealousy made me this
What I am today,
I said out loud that
I am very proud,
To be on the top rather in the crowd.

*

One motivation changed my life
I thought it was a hanging knife

Which killed me to build my creation
I will always remember that motivation.

*

This is the first poem that I had written. And I know I have come a long way.

There are only a few words if spoken at the right times and at the right place that ignite the fire in you to do things that you thought were beyond your capacity.

I started this not because I was good at it but because someone challenged a small part of me or maybe I did get influenced by the praises the others were getting. I wanted to be selfish too but it took me a long time to understand that all this is not for me but for the people who are moved by reading what I write. **Kind of becoming their motivation, I guess. Maybe I am overdoing it now.**

2. Here they come again

I thought you were gone
But I was completely wrong.
I was prepared for you,
Still was a little scared of you.

*

I was waiting for you
On the front door,
But you entered from the back,
I waited for some time,
Still, you were completely black.

*

I knew nothing,
However, I had to write,
Stepping back at that moment,
Was not feeling quite right.

*

I had faced you earlier,
This time you were harder,
You have seen me earlier,
But this time I was smarter.

*

I wrote and wrote
Whatever I knew,

I was knowing I will
Only get a few.

*

Seeing my friends after exams,
They were cool,
I thought only I was scared and was a big fool.

*

That was the only feared thing in school days and now when I look back, **they were mere checkpoints that were to be crossed.** It was a big deal to me back then but now they do not have that control over me. It may be the same for you too.

3. Earth

Being round and round
Weighing pound and pound
Always helping us a lot
Making no sighing sound.
*

Waking us up for school
Walking around the sun,
But you are still cool
Making our daily work run.
*

No matter what we all do
You always stay fit
Sometimes our greediness
Makes you ugly and unfit.
*

Showing your anger
Is not your duty
But it is us and only us
To protect your beauty
*

Flowers and rains
Make us forget our pains
Smell the earth at least once

Lend you a priceless gain.
*

Smoke and dirt around
Make you crazy, it sounds
When you show your anger
People worship on their grounds.
*

Earth thanks for all
Waking me up and helping
Giving place on your lap
Making trees and fruits ripen.
*

Maybe it is a last-call
From you and me
To make them aware
As they would fall.
*

I do not have any idea what made me write this. Maybe on a certain day, my mind was like **'Are we really deserving of this nature that has been offering us things from the times as far back as one can remember?'**
It hits the right spot when you think about it from your mind too.

4. Summer is here

It has arrived as usual
Finally, the days are hot
Summer is already here
In a perfect blow spot.

*

Holidays are back here,
We are curious 'maybe more'
We enjoy a punishment
Of one and only furious sun.

*

Trips and tours set off
Challenged by strong winds
Someone just gets off
to buy some cold drinks.

*

Being at home all alone
No friends indeed
How to enjoy vacations?
Friends help we need.

*

Boring days and nights
Eating, sleeping, burning
All our unnecessary fights

We cry by remembering.

*

It is going to last
A month or two
After that enjoying
By chatting with you…!

*

The place from where I come from the Sun is out to really get you and get you hard. There are always things about this season that no other can beat. Firstly, are the mangoes in the heat and holidays we used to get. **Now I feel nostalgic because I will never be able to see this season with the same curious eyes and mind once again.**

5. It is Me

I was like a clown
Always up and down
No stability at all
I would always fall.
*

Some made me feel bad
But some were glad
I thought I was nothing
But I am a lazy lad.
*

Got friends like angels
Made me fly high
Without whom today
I only deeply sigh.
*

Calling them up
When they are busy
Talking nonsense things
Was always very easy.
*

When they hung up
I often nearly cried
Thinking about them

Always I have tried.
*

Maybe they moved on
Leaving me alone
But will always wait
Till they are back home.
*

Saying goodbye
Was not right
I said see you soon
But they were quiet.
*

When they ignored
I thought it was okay
But when it continued
I was like "HEY!"
*

They are all gone
Leaving me alone
It is time to say bye
And I know it is my last lie.
*

I have always grounded and humbled myself by depreciating whatever I was getting from others. Maybe it is a coping mechanism that makes me strong enough to face the times when I am alone.

Of course, you are going to be happy when everyone is around you but do you really feel content when you are on your own? That is the thing to think about not just once but twice.

6. Being Unique

Education is learning
Not skillfully memorizing
Its path is never-ending
Seems probably suffering.
*

Knowledge for all
It is a never-ending call
Only reading and writing
Bring us fame and all.
*

There is a hurtless pain
To do something unique
But there is no way
To combine both techniques.
*

Satisfaction is priority
But life chooses the majority
Chances are more here
All goes wrong there.
*

All walk on smooth roads
No one wants to be pricked
The bushy path is good

One which is never picked.

*

Do what you like the most
Not what others hope
Be successful one day
Success that they cannot cope with.

*

It is another way of telling you to choose the other path. Not any other path that you see but the path where you think you will enjoy the journey more than reaching the tip of that and achieving the goal. We copy from people around us, that is accepted human nature we are all built like that, but there is surely something inside us that makes us completely different from what we are trying to be. You must find that thing sooner or later.

7. She is quite different

Something was odd
That day I believe
Something unusual
I wanted to receive
*

She was one among them
With whom I did not speak
She smiled in my dreams
Suddenly I used to be awake
*

Never dared to talk to her
But still tried with guts
And mind always said
"Are you gone nuts?"
*

We smiled at each other
Simply maybe for fun
Slowly all turned to
Relationship of short run.
*

We used to talk rarely
Never crossed our ends
Maybe we knew that

We were just good friends!
*

The school came to an end
Final talks and memories
And I still sigh daily
'She was only a good friend.'
*

There is that aura about the school crushes that we carry all our lives. It is meant for us to understand that there is a thing called **"Childish Love"** to which we all must surrender. It is a good thing because you learn that a good thing will only last for a certain time and what has come has to go but you cannot accept it at that moment because you think you are in love.

8. Why only me?

The day is bad
Maybe not the evening
Teachers scold me
And go on blaming.

*

My morale is down
Heartbeats low
Writing the poems
Really slow and slow.

*

Being happy and frolicking
Makes me very glad
Being scolded always
Makes me really sad.

*

Thoughts are running
In my restless brain
I will be lonely and happy
Never put any strain.

*

Friends too laugh
But that is fine
I do not have one

There are only nine

*

Promised me that
I will always care
My happiness and rest
Which is very rare.

*

"The days are bad not our luck, but it depends on us how we take it"

How a simple thing affects you till the core that you start to care for your mental health or at least when you are that young. It might be a silly thing to me now but that would have been a great deal at that time. Maybe life is much easier when you look at it in the third person after some years of wisdom.

9. Poet's life

No worries and aches
Knowledge of words
Can make a way
Through situation worse.
*

State of mind being cool
Talking to myself
No one to make me fool
Being with oneself.
*

Writing and thinking
Was always a passion
To bring it to life
It was a big tension.
*

Stress-free, cool life
I wanted to live
Nobody of them accepted
And said to me to leave.
*

Studies are good
But not to me
Academics are everything

They said to me.

*

Lost between myself
My brain and heart
If you do not study
You will pull a cart.

*

Poet dies and gets reborn
But nobody cares
My success is most
Of them do not share.

*

But I am happy
And he was and is
A great poet or will be
One day at least.

*

When I started writing better, better than some broken words with no meaning, I realized that it is not easy to find a way to make it happen and to make it big in a day. **I sit and laugh now because I write very few pieces compared to when I started.**
You too feel the same thing, when you start something that is considered out of the box everything and anything turns against you just to make you realize that if you can do it, can you give your everything doing it?

10. The Tide that Brings Happiness

Away from chaos
There is a way
No better than heaven, for the soul
A place that justifies you
Makes you, more yours.
*

When the tiny sand particles
Got stuck in my foot
The sun went below the horizon
And the tide had just left shore
This all was my heaven.
*

Sat on a small dune
Thinking of one
Seeing through the clear sky
The reddish-orange appearance!
I wanted her on my side.
*

I clenched some sand
And closed my eyes
We would remain together
That made me curious

Her hand was in my hand now
*

Though the closed eyes flickered a bit
But the palm didn't resist her presence
The breeze hugged me going along
And the tide touched my feet
Which completed my love song.
*

From the heaven still, the angels come
To complete a wish of heartbroken
After her death, my life was not mine
But only her death was mine.
*

You have only a moment
Say whatever, you want to
It is never too late to love someone
Even in their absence
They are with you, being in all.
*

Losing someone very close to your heart takes a part of you as well. A part, that was never yours but given to you and you accepted it as yours. You were never complete before and now, when they are gone, you will never be complete either. **They made you what you always wanted to be, fulfilled.** Soon that void will catch you, freeze your thoughts and you will never be free again. The only thing you could do is to accept the fact that they are gone and at least when they were going, they were only yours and always had been. So, cheer up and smile, look at the night sky see what it has to say to you, maybe already you know what it says… I LOVE YOU.

• 22 •

11. The Old House

An old house looked younger
As the dust storm had it
A small light of hope
Had blinked for, no years to fit
*

The build rather looked shattered
Hearing the locks creaking
Cracks on the dinner plate
The cutlery is too freaking.
*

Window closed, doors too
The keyhole gave a picture
Of the vast land in it
In the imagination of a creature
*

Small safe, photo kept above
Of the most loved, it had
The lock was ill and rusted
With life's all sad
*

Safe had got nothing
Nothing but the feeling of love
The old house still waits

For the storm to stop, there sits a dove.

*

The old house here is the heart that has waited too long to feel something. It has seen it all yet it waits, it longs for the one thing it wants to be what it was meant to be. The heart that waits for love craves it in everything and sometimes the wait seems to be endless.

We do not realize what we are missing till it somehow completes us. And then, we understand the essence of patience and the longing for love. We are not clear on what to make of the puzzle till the last piece, the most loved one, completes it.

12. Should we cry?

Hold the sand in your palms
It slips as fast as time
Only traces remain within
Not the lively rhymes
[Know what you have]

*

Leaves fall off, they turn yellow
Though the tree loses its beauty
To bring up the new ones
As the part of nature treaty
[Nature is final]

*

We encourage the butterfly
For its color and flightless fight
But what about the cocoon stage
Wasn't it hard? Though it fights
[See efforts before results]

*

The fist of clouds around the Sun
Cannot stop it is a dark-less gleam
It finds a way to swim
All through the world unseen
[Make way in hard times]

*

The hatred between warm and cool
Often gives us an uplift to live
And we believe it is just a part of nature
Following simultaneously to live
[Balance your life]

*

Flowers think they are the beauty
Not those green leaves
Leaves think we support and bow low
When we quit the flower doesn't live
[Think and believe]

*

Man sees all these small things
Which are largely apparent to him
Thinks he is the smartest creature
And thinks, the light of Nature is Dim.

*

There are hundreds of messages hidden in plain sight from which we can learn but we are too ignorant to see beyond something or too close to forget that we have a nose too. **When we understand the essence of things, we appreciate things that make us what we should have been already.**

13. The Travel

Race of life never ends
Our efforts to make it better
Continues to persuade it
To make a better leader
*

We often make the proper decision
It is but not that perfect
We indeed are made to insight
The vision to give an impact
*

The travel goes on
Where the rainbow ends
Where the oceans end
But it stops when we bend
*

Learn to sacrifice yourself
For the construction of your destiny
Learn to fall and support
For the betterment of your entity
*

Be responsible to lead
Be honorable to take a loss
Be calm to listen

And be the critic to choose

*

Never think it is enough
Make it better and better
Because no one can make it perfect
Only one can make it best later

*

Farewell starts when you end your work
Do not stop till everything is completed
Farewell should be delayed till death
And should be given, not Pleaded.

*

Travelling makes you think does this bliss ever end? We have nothing to make of it just be there. One's search does not complete when he travels the whole world but when he sees what is inside him that is yet to be discovered. There is a world that constantly changes based on your thoughts. **Do you really know yourself that well that every corner of your heart and soul needs and demands only one thing?**

14. From the Dim lights

All over the world
Lies the happiness, hidden
Souls wandering to find a home
A home that has peace and love
One in which they could rest
From the darkness of the world
*

I see the wanderers
Losing their homes, where they were brought
To find a better place in the world
They leave their sinful body
And are found elsewhere
In the dim light of heaven, they think
*

My sound thereafter follows them
In the sequence of good and bad
The path traveled by everyone
But neither seeing nor felt
Souls go on and meet some more
And there, the soul gets an end
With no joy and peace.
*

Many faces people show

But their soul is not justified,
Threatened from the world's appreciation
Faces frighten me
Betrayal, sin, vituperation, all in one.

*

There are many things beyond our reach. People do not think about what is beyond all this they just follow what is already written. **Everyone has different characters. Many faces are hidden in one.** Each layer of one's personality comes out as per the situation and that is why it is harder for us to sometimes identify them. A person with selfless interest does not exist.

Even when you see yourself acting from a third-person perspective, you will also understand why some people hate you and people who want to be with you.

15. Then to Now

Afraid of the dark, lived alone
Along the way
Just walked alone
*

From time to time
Good changed to bad
And bad to worse
No chance of a smoothen road
The roads got rougher
*

Days, weeks, and months
I have been waiting for you
Walking towards the destiny
Never saw that
'How beautiful the path was'
*

Didn't knew
The path and destiny were the same
Never saw through the darkness
To the bright light of hope
*

Before the word seemed endless
But now my world

'It is only you.... '

*

You find yourself going down the same lane which you subconsciously think is made for you. You do not see the circumstances or the consequences. **You overcome them.** When you believe something is right for you, you do not stop or change paths. You make your journey and goals into one. And sometimes, you will understand that your journey teaches you more than the goal. **The goal is just for the satisfaction, the real things you will learn are from the roads you take to reach there.**

16. No One

Nobody cares
Who am I?
Should I be alive?
Or should I die?
*

No one to look after
No one, even to talk
Life is quite boring
Alone I have to walk
*

Trees and birds
Are they closest friends?
No one can break
And no one can bend
*

Life has many turns
One of them is now
I have to move forward
Though being slow
*

I had to laugh
Also, crying alone
No friends left

Not even my clone

*

It is all about
Bitter but good
I know my friend
How they really look.

*

There are times when you are quite foolish to not see that the only person that can help you to get out of any situation is the person you see in the mirror. **The only hand you must hold is yours and only yours.** The poem is not about how lonely you are and have no one to help you, but to understand that feeling low just because no one is there is not the right thing. You must understand that the things you owe yourself are far greater than the interest of others. So, believe in yourself because only you know that you can do it and how to do it.

17. I miss you

I was not that famous
But surely was a part
You are and will be you
I was at last in my friends' chart
*

No one was caring
It was only you
But you too changed
And said, "Who are you?"
*

I was really sad then
Decided to move on
But your memories
Told me to hold on
*

That day when I
Was in no mood
Your smile made
My day good
*

These funny things
When you are gone
I still remember

And regret being alone

*

A friend like you
'Not really a friend!'
But a relationship
Which will never end

*

I thought of you
I really felt you
Now because of your smile
I cannot forget you

*

I am still waiting for you
You too come along
Let's turn this thing
A way 'more' long.

*

I know it is very silly not to use those words to describe such a worthy feeling but that is what love is all about, **it is innocent, it is better kept hidden, it is pure.** It is always complicated when only one among the two is deeply in love. I know heartbreaks can be bitter but living in the shadows and loving a person can really make you feel claustrophobic!

18. Long time no see

I hope you still
Remember my name
I am empty although
By getting all the fame
*

You and me are alike
The cherished cuteness
What you have is not the same
I still remember your madness
*

Your art is beyond
This whole world
It makes me happy
Even your hair curled
*

I felt a little lonely
Till you came into my life
Now you are an inspiration
For me to read and write
*

We had some fights
Even ignored each other
But we're friends and

Will be friends forever

*

I had not thought
One day I will write to you
But now I had written
And will always care for you.

*

This was written for a very special person.
There are a few relationships in this world that cannot be justified by words. These relationships with them are so spontaneous that after some time you really forget how we really met them. But the memories we shared, and the fun we had engraved a mark on our souls and can never be changed no matter what.
We all have that person with whom we were close for a very short period but their role had a great impact on us. Cheers to them for making our lives less miserable.

19. I hated that time

My heart was broken
Not once, but several times
Then I stood for a chance
To make this relationship rhyme
*

Stood and had an early fall
Made me heartless
I got new suggestions
To opt for the way of friendliness
*

From days till now
I never had a fall
Searching for someone
Making memories recall
*

I fell apart that day
But I am 'still' no?
Friends are my life
And I am going a little slow
*

To capture moments
Always, I had waited
You are a great fool

Others all stated

*

I always lived for others
But nobody bothered
They used me as a thing
For which they ordered

*

I was counting
My last breath
I thought they would come
To see their friend wreck

*

Nobody came
I waited for them
They all found stones
But forever lost a gem.

*

It is a give-and-take world. We make contacts instead of making friends. We use them and they do just the same. Any relationship today is not the same anymore. Meanings have changed, people have changed and the rules of this 'game' have changed too. We all take part in this and then blame each other because there is no other way of doing it. **There are people in today's world who are here to get you down into the rubble with them just because they have not seen a bird fly high above.**

20. Sleep Eat and Repeat

The days have finally come
Where I can only enjoy
No studies, no reading
No Julius, Nor Helen of Troy
*

The summer is set on
Making us feel sweaty
If we have an AC
Then we are lucky
*

New foods to try
All the other stuff too
Making our self-drowsy
With a shake or two
*

Schools are closed
Traveling now starts
Meeting our siblings
Living in other parts
*

Moving out feels good
Playing all day and night
Never getting exhausted

And ending with the fight.

*

As a child, I was waiting for the summer season to come by because summer for us was 'Freedom'. **There is no work at all, everything slows down a bit and everything tastes good in summer.**

It was a holiday I guess that I have written this with the words that were at the top of my head. I know it is not the essence of summer completely but can make you nostalgic for sure.

21. Changed

I am left lonely
Forever once again
Without love and care
But with lots of pain

*

I lost her
I think forever
Smiles have stopped
For once are over

*

Everyone said to live
As it was month and more
I was left alone
And quite bored

*

A secret hidden in my heart
Which never comes out
It will stay always there
The thing that I never talk about

*

We lose or win
We have something
Today I lost me

Most precious thing

*

I have to change
Wrong things all along
If I did not do it
I will regret it lifelong

*

Changes take place
Even if there is a change in time
We will be together
And you will be mine.

*

Even the smallest change in the person you are in love with, affects you till the core. You know they have changed, by the way they talk, they behave, they act around you. There are different things that change in your surroundings but you notice only the things that matters. Your life evolves around these changes.

22. Chattering

Talking all the day
Never get bored
Using all the energy
Rather than keeping it stored
*

Blah blah blah
We used to chatter
Giving result to
Each and every matter
*

Friends departed
When we used to talk
Chattering in the class
Which was a greater task
*

No secrets hidden
All are out now
It is spread to everyone
Like a bloody blow
*

Sometimes we talk alone
Regretting our own Falls things
If we know ourselves

It will surely give us wings.
*

Talking makes us feel good
But no one understands
Especially teachers and parents
We have to take a stand
*

It is really fun
To be a chatterbox
By being more talkative
All the feelings unlock
*

Be talkative
If you actually are
Can take your imagination
Really very far.
*

I know that the more you talk the more collisions of thoughts you have, rather than creating a thought you carry someone else's as one of yours.

You put your heart out while doing it, it hides your insecurities well I can give you that. We are meant to talk, to communicate, and also are made to bear the consequences it brings with it.

"A smile can say a thousand words but a thousand words if understood, have more weight than the smile bears".

23. Boring

A day with no play
It is like hell to me
This day is boring
Only I sigh, you see

*

Nothing is going right
All things are churning
No poems this time
As the thoughts are burning

*

Left with pen and book
Started writing stories
Using the killer time
Turned it into glories

*

Suggestions are good
But I couldn't take up
Chatting all the day
And saying what is up?

*

I am not the murderer
To kill the bloody time
Instead, use the energy

To make things mine

*

We all feel bored
Then somehow manage it
I am quite a lazy lad
Yeah, but a little bit

*

Got a poem to write
Sitting on the floor
I would complete it
And soon feel bored.

*

Boredom, for me, usually creates an opportunity to be productive. When I sit idle the thoughts in my mind start churning up and they collide to let out a spark. **A creation out of curiosity is completely different from a creation that comes out of boredom.** Our mind works in mysterious ways, when it is bored and has nothing to do, it comes up with words that align perfectly, to give it meaning that takes a lot to comprehend it.

24. Happy writing

For me, it should be my career
Usually, no one supports
I will not lose the hope
Till I make it a helping boat
*

Being rich with money
Is the trending fashion
But being a poet
Is my favorite passion
*

Read and smile and laugh
Reading my silly words
I think it is better to be a poet
Then being those jerky nerds
*

Friends change my view
On expressing my feelings
Through the poetic forms
On my successful dealings
*

Then I started to write
Finding some new words
Being, unique and all

One, among the poetic lords.

*

It is funny to be a writer
It is not said by me
But others usually say
And make me flee

*

Still deciding on my future
To be a writer or not
I write my poems
Without any crazy plot

*

'I enjoy my life always
More than causing a threat
We should enjoy it now
Because we may be dead'.

*

As of now, I do not think I have reached a level where I can perceive it as an option. That is what friends do to you, they make the mountain seem small.

These things apart, how funny it is to read someone's work when you do not even know what he or she has gone through to write that. **A reader's perspective is always different from the writer's.**

What good does it bring when the words you choose do not change in the readers' minds?

25. Time pass

Nothing to do
Is the main thing
We pass the time
By only thinking

*

Every time we say
We will do it later
And still, we love
To be a work hater

*

Do something new
To get the success
And get married
To our beloved princess

*

Time always matters
In everything we do
In love, in hatred
And in friendship too

*

We have hobbies
Which we carry now
To pass the time

And get a mighty blow

*

Time is very powerful
We have always learned
One who doesn't respect it
He gets easily burnt

*

Eat, enjoy, and repeat
Pass the time easily
But be careful
You can lose it completely.

*

No matter what anyone says we all enjoy a long break from what we are doing. There is a special quality only in us to do things that are completely absurd in the times when we can actually make a difference. But that is just how the human mind works, especially ours. **Since there is time to kill why not procrastinate things till it becomes a burden and we question our life.** That is something about a "mid-life crisis" because you are just passing the time.

26. It is Raining

I stepped out
It started raining
I didn't stop there
Just went on walking
*

The mother nature
Recreated the world
On the tip of mountains
The droplets swirled
*

My black jacket
Was on me
My hat didn't let me
But I clearly see
*

I put my head down
To smell the earthy rain
It refreshed me
And relieved me of pain
*

Those bloody pains
I hated them
Saw a pearl on the leaf

And caught that then

*

I thought to be here
It was a new earth
I looked up and down
And felt it was a heart

*

I sat on a bench
I was cool and I just
Thought of writing a poem
But couldn't do it!

*

As the drops hit the earth, they not only touch the soil but also your soul. All your pain washes away, everything that is black turns white. Inside your head, you change. All your senses are open to change by the rain. All your vulnerabilities are not there anymore. They do not exist.
Rain hides everything within itself be it you or your soul.

27. Met after a long time

It is been so long
That I have seen you
We met again today
With no hint or clue
*

You read my poems
I am very glad
You didn't believe
Thought of me as a lad
*

You look so cute
As you always were
I became a bit ugly
With sadness in there
*

You always smile
When you see me
I changed my mood
I know… you see
*

You come and go
Usually, I do not care
But sigh in my heart

Which I show is quite rare
*

I want to say the truth
I really want to know
What do you think about me?
Say out loud, do not be low
*

We meet each other
Saying only 'hello'
I only stare at you
Really an idiot fellow
*

You know me
How I really am…
Being a dumb
But completely calm
*

It is time to go back again
This time a Bub-Bye
It is an ugly feeling
Where I sigh.
*

When you are deeply in love, they are your addiction. You want them around you all the time. In fact, sometimes, you miss them so much that you do not even realize you are hurting yourself. A few things change in your life, and you do not seem to care but anything that changes in that person it affects you. It bothers you. You do not want to lose them, you crave them, and you have nothing without them. But it is not true, isn't it?

When you detach yourself from them you know that it was the time that made you vulnerable and here, I am going against my own feelings.

28. The Goodbye

Be with you soon
All the time I will miss you
When you are far away
I think I am in a different world
Filled with sadness, but curious to meet you the next day

*

You make everyone happy
But not me
Because your effortless love
Takes my breath away to you
My hearts pound with love

*

I wait for you and your goodbye
Till you have made my day
This action may have love
The sweet gesture of your
'Goodbye,' you say

*

'See you soon again'
Faster than the wave washes the shore
Then the wind through leaves
Than the blink of an eye
As the earth cries to rain for more

*

A small dew on the leaf
Looks like a pearl over it
A small gesture- Bye!
Makes my lips widen enough
To confine you in it.

*

I think of you the rest of the day
Am I rude to you?
Do you even like me?
At last, I get a confirmation
By that 'Goodbye" of you.

*

Goodbyes have always been a bad experience for me because it creates a void in me that takes a long time to fill or disappear. Especially, when it is a person, the emptiness is significant. It is really loud. You cannot shut it, because that gap is not filled by replacing that person with that thing.

'See you soon,' they say, but do they know that how helpless and hopeless we feel when they are not around? Situations like these test your patience to wait for them to be back, for that time to back.

29. Frustration

Everybody in the world
Have some cacophonies going on?
Their minds blocked by norms
Always have a dead-end
Just a marathon of bookworms
*

The more things you gulp
You are the Great
The greatness will not lie
It is the truth that will take you aback
A race like this continues till you die
*

There is a place in your heart
Where all these frustrations grow
THE HUMANITY OF THE FUTURE
Leads on abandoned plain
Plains where there are no dreams to sow
*

But that is not the end
It is just the start of an evil mind
To make the world
Poorer for life
And love hatred more blind

*

Ends with the suicide
The pressure exceeds the patience
Who cares what you bear
Not studies that make you
It is your passion, making less fear

*

Frustration is a state of mind
It is repugnant against all
Clear your thoughts and talk out loud
Find life in every moment
Not moments in your small life.

*

How frustrated you are because the narrow alleys in your minds never let you free and give you a way to achieve something. You are in debt for your not-doings. You could have gotten up and gone far and yet you chose to stay and do nothing about it. The fire in you burns still. You have the power and the resources to make it. You must forge your own paths and your own journey to the goals.

"There is no better feeling than to be on top and rest when you have achieved everything that you ever dreamed of."

30. A Dream

His finger, you hold
In any situation of danger
He covers you with his care
'You are my shadow' he says
Follow in the dark as the glare

*

A flare he gave you to choose.
To become what you always wanted to
Never get depressed
Never get carried away
By what someone says to you

*

Your father had a dream
He never accomplished either
All the factors stood against him
But he had a small hope
That small hope is you, that ignite his dim

*

Some dreams are harder to follow
Not because it is hard
But your dreams face the obstacle
It is the hurdle which fits your leg
And makes your intuition, retard.

*

There is a word, 'combine'
Combine and play the games
Dreams are not one
And neither the hopes
Stand up and be a unique one

*

Create a world of success
Everyone can taste it
Every eye filled and hands stretched
For all the glory drizzling
From which their throats quenched.

*

Father, I know your dreams
But what about Mine?
Aren't they a small part of you?
How can I go against you?
By all the power, I get from you

*

He would have surely said this…
'My dreams are part of yours
And the power I give, are my dreams
You use your strengths
I am an old man to fulfill your dreams
If you accomplish your dreams
They complete mine too.'

*

Our fathers had a dream which they could not achieve because they were busy raising us and making a living for us. They project those dreams on us. They see themselves in us, achieving the things that they would have if the circumstances were a bit more favorable for them. And, we think that they are forcing us to do things that we do not like or are good at. It is not really a hopeless situation because when you are a parent you want to make your child's life good.

Can you think why will they not project their dreams on you when their whole life they have thought that that thing will give them the satisfaction of living? Don't you think they want you to be satisfied with your life?

Can you understand his agony?

31. The Unlucky friend

Alone in the darkness,
Even the tears start to cry
The voice gets low
But then someone holds you
The strength that you get by only a few
*

Hopes of light twinkle
Even in that mind
The mind of an unlucky fellow
To stand and face
What is the destiny left behind?
*

Lies gamble with the game
The game of trust and betrayal
The truth left unsaid
From that unlucky fellow
Who had just got lives trial
*

That one person says
Do not worry I will shield
Shield the double-faced Lie
Betray, it is darkness
And glow you with my light

*

Everyone does not get that person
But the unlucky fellow did
He got someone to share his loneliness
With all hearts and faith
The fellow got a friendliness

*

You were not an unlucky fellow
Just deprived of love and care
I wanted to help you
And you were my friend (she said)
An unlucky friend (sighed the boy)

*

She did not return then
Though he was not lonely now
She gave him a reason to live
Of her memories
Of which he dreams to live.

*

You have heard people telling you not to rely on someone for your own happiness because when the person leaves, you are just left with the memories of theirs to live with. Sometimes you have only one reason to look up to and live your life. **The Memories.** You feel it as if it all happened just yesterday.

32. The Bond that we have

You may break the promise
Which I in turn will keep
In all the hollow vessels of mine
Those statements will run wild
The promise made is very deep

*

'Trust,' the word is enough
You have your care upon me
Thought I must recheck on you at times
Because I worry
But do not show up easily

*

When, back in time we had met
Destiny had a setup for us
Something strange and unusual
Which we now find in our bond
Being together was the principle

*

Truth, Trust, and Time
Made us get close
Almighty bless us from above
Thus, concluding his tale

Add a few hearts that never get froze
*

To you, I write that I could not say
Life is not long to betray
Time is not left to slay
Promise is not broken to stay
And our hearts are not together to play
*

I entitle you to my wish
I write you in my poems
Do I never send it to you?
Because some hearts have fear
Of losing someone precious like you
*

The Bond that we have
We will have it till our ends
Warmth of sunshine
And the chill of the dark knight
Splash of rain
And fallen leaves of autumn
Will make my heart fulfilled.
*

Your heart is filled with feelings of a person so deep that whatever you write or talk about or do you think of them add them to your life even when they are not around. Is it not love? Is it not obsession? Is it not for them you do not want to get up in the mornings or write poetries? And, yeah, those butterflies never go out of order till you fall in love again and again with the same person.

How subtle is it to not say love but bond when you know that the one word you want to say may be the reason that you might lose them?

33. Pressure

The exams are near
Read and write well
Practice all the day
Parents often tell
*

You failed to score
It is not your fault
We can win again
Ignoring all taunt
*

Do not lose hope
Even if you lose twice
Learn from mistakes
Which will make you wise
*

Do not blame your fate
You will get what you need
Remember one thing that
Increase your learning speed
*

Not only academics
Can do all for you
But your instincts

Can make things do
*

I will not say you
Just read and write
Things you are interested
Will make you bright
*

Choose your life
Instead of pressure
It is one in seven billion
I have some pleasure
*

Do what you want?
Never sigh after that
Be unique in all
Not just a confused brat.
*

As you grow up you understand that this pressure affects the least. Many things make you fall twice and rise only once. There was a time we all felt that pressure on our shoulders to prove something and once you have done it, **it either becomes useless or unnecessary.**

34. Inner Voice

I heard someone
Within my soul
Are they, my thoughts?
Playing a major role

*

'Do something different!'
The calm voice said
Making me get up
And shake my head

*

Soon I got to know
It was my 'inner voice'
Showing me the path
Clearing my ideas twice

*

What I can do?
That is the question for me
It replied with the phrase
'Help me, to search me'

*

I frowned at hearing
The voice became a bit stiff
I glared at thoughts

There is no place for 'if'

*

'Listen to yourself
Do not be carried away
It is about you and your fate
Not your family or bae.

*

Now I really knew
For what I have come for
Making all the things happen
Things which I long for.

*

I talk to him now
All the days
He suggests ideas
Making all the possible ways.

*

Have you ever noticed that your inner voice can never raise its loudness but it certainly raises the spirits, brightens up ideas, and pushes you through the times of dark. We all talk with ourselves about things that we have done or the things that have happened to us.

Your inner voice is often right. It is your gut feeling. Call it intuition or sixth sense or anything for that sake.

35. Proud or Guilty

All the men at the border
Shed their blood
They even save hostages
From 'quakes and floods
*

They leave their homes
And live miles apart
Are they immigrants?
Or do we play in human parts?
*

A billion and a quarter
People are saved
If there is no peace
Always they are blamed!
*

I have a lot of pressure
We always blame
Handling political pressure
Is not always the same
*

Will they die on borders?
Their families were keen
After the respectful death

The family gets a stitching machine'
*

I salute the army men
Who are ready to die!
I will not let them down
By a political lie
*

Let them do what
They think is right
Not from anguish-ness
But their plants fight
*

Those inhumans are not
My brothers and sisters
Who throws stones at you?
Who save them from sinister?
*

They think they can
Break our unity
But one thing I will say
One day, you will be guilty
*

I regret that till today
I could not help my army
But today I take an oath
To serve my country and army!
*

We all see it in the news and those times were difficult for us all. The subconscious registered those acts and did nothing but when we think about that it really mattered to speak out. **But the powerless human like me could have done only so much.**

But now the times are changing, we know what we are doing. Serve them with solving the internal conflicts rather than pointing the fingers at them.

36. What do you want in return?

Some gifts are given
In the hopes of being returned
That one was special
Returning makes feelings better

*

A special occasion was held
And I gave him the value
Which he would surely
Return without any clue

*

I went to him and handed
The better one, I could buy
What do you want in return?
He asked and said goodbye

*

He always said 'See you soon'
But it was his special day
So, I shut myself and sobbed
A Sun, without his hay

*

The next day we usually talked
Like the day one

Neither of us were bothered
About dream gift fun

*

He laughed, I laughed
We were frolicking all day
The same question repeated
'What do you want in return?'

*

I was sad and feeling guilty
For a slipshod then
He counted his gifts
'One, two… six, and ten!'

*

Sometimes gifts are not only things that are given.
Sometimes there are feelings attached to it. Sometimes we
expect, we wait for the favor to be returned. Sometimes gifts
mark the value of the bond and sometimes they are mere
gifts.
Everything that you lend a person out of love and kindness is
a gift.
**"Do gifts really matter or do the feelings matter, with
which they are given?"**

37. The Undesirable Secret

It is not just a secret
The whole world lies within
Those few lines are hidden
Inside me like a sin

*

Sometimes those words are uttered
To one who can understand
But at last, are very feeble
And intolerable to withstand

*

I reach a state of blackout
When that feeling sickens me
Makes me write, rather than shout
Or else burdens the whole body

*

Some statements are to be told
Some are kept as secrets
This was one of my secrets
Which was to be 'untold'

*

Feelings are to be expressed
Not to be hidden within and die

I thought the lines
And end up with a 'convincing lie'

*

Talk to someone or write
Tell them the things you feel
The thing you know
But I make my thoughts kneel

*

This truth will go with me
To the heaven of human
Till then I would kill myself
And be one of 'Human'

*

A lie with love
Buried deep in my heart
Need a pure soul to explain
Or else I cannot

*

On this planet, I will not find a soul
To share all these secrets
These are only for me
These are my 'undesirable secrets.'

*

There are things that only you understand. It might be a silly
thing but it's your secret to be kept within yourself.
"They will never get it!"

We all have certain secrets which will not be shared but will go with us. it is our insecurities that do not allow us to share them. The fear of judgment leads to hiding the talks, hence they become your secrets and only yours to keep.

38. Betrayal

Vituperation routed from nowhere
Following came jealousy with it
Jealousy of proving themselves better
Stated in a perfect way as
'Friendship has competition in it'
*

Break a relationship that stabs you
It slowly creeps at first
Spreads poison in one's mind
Poison of ego and jealousy
And then gives brutal stab from behind
*

The word friend blindfolds trust
Does not allow us to see the light of truth
The thought weaves with
Seed of hazardous love and care
And you still think 'Was it fair?'
*

No one understood better than them
The meaning of trust and loyalty
The brotherhood binding them
Above love, above everything existing
Once brotherhood had clarity.

*

I know you trust some people blindly but people have their own conscience. When their benefit outweighs yours there might be a slight bend towards rewards that suits them on the cost of your trust. Of course, they will not do it in a moment but time changes, and things change too.
There are only a few things that can hurt us and those are the things we love. Most of the time. Maybe because we remember them for a longer time.
Whom will you trust,
'A blind man with a sword or A man with just a smile?'

39. A Common friend

A smile can turn into a desire
Touch can turn into trust
But not as a common friend
It is just formal at first
The leading eye contacts
With some words to exchange
And the cheeks turn red
In a pinkish-red range
Clenched by the thought of losing
I was partly silent
Partly because it hurts
When your brain and heart are equivalent
Not having you, your laugh
My lips were packed
Heart said many out loud
Diminished words, though bounced back
Life makes every turn a 'u'
Arguing with me to leave
You are not for her, though...
That 'thought' makes me believe
'Should I say her...'
The words would disappear after
I do not know in which sands

But only echoing thereafter
At last, one day our eyes met
We smiled or maybe not
Alone in our world of thoughts
And soon our hands caught
With the blush, she turned
I thought I would rather lose her today
But I would surely say it
"Will you be my common friend" without any delay
That is what she expected
Because still we are together
Sharing all the things we need to do
Only as a common friend of each other.
Well, well, well… Are not we familiar with situations like these. Trust me, they hit harder than the little finger hitting the edge of the table.
The mere dilemma of letting them know the feelings that you are hiding just to have some moments with them without the obvious awkwardness.
There is an upside to it is that they are forever yours to have but the only downside is that not in the sense and manner you want to have them in your life.

40. That is what I feel

No matter how harsh the time was
Standing beside me was my love, You!
Love that beholds me to be passionate
That says I am here for you
*

We did not talk a lot
Neither do we meet often
Though I felt you around
Was that my love, actually?
*

For sometimes our heart stood silent
Nor does it approach you
Neither felt love for the others
Was as silent as a leaf with the dew
*

Did she leave me?
My heart was keen to know
But did the same as you
Moved on with whatever was left now
*

It dreamt of many things
One among which was to work a long way
Overcoming jealousy with trust and faith

Spending with you, the whole time of the day

*

What I dreamt did not matter
What I felt was nothing
Though crossed the paths
We could not feel our hearts rotting

*

But then the time came
I could not bear 'a dead heart'
I took a step for you
Making my heart sweet, not tart

*

My heart cringed
It thought he lost you again
I was taken aback and felt
'From where did this all began?'

*

It finds itself guilty
From the past of its sins
Rose from where it had fallen
I have not looked back ever since

*

Whenever eyes met finally
There was a big smile on your face
I thought you felt me
Which fastened my heart's pace

*

We laughed at each other
And felt 'why did we do that?'
I felt for you and you for me
More than talks, our eyes had much for chat.

*

There is always a contradiction in love.
How do you know whether the person is the right one for you? And who really is the 'right one?'
They say, 'When you cannot be with the person but love them truly that is real love,' But if it was really meant to be then why are we not together?
People who lost in love make such contradictions against the ones who got what they always wanted the love of their life.
People who lose often create an idea of acceptance of pain by justifying the unjust nature of their life for love.
So, if it is true that you do not end up with the person you truly love, then is it even real when you do end up with them?
Quite a dilemma, thanks to the broken heart.

41. It is only you

It is only you whom I remember
All the time when you are away
I am lucky to have you
A person filled with love
And hatred against the anger
*

All I know is only you
Now on whom I can rely upon
Could share things with you
Feel that I never experienced
Before meeting you
*

You feel lucky with me
Have you ever thought
That is what I think
And whom do I care?
It is only you for me.
*

Dawn without the song of birds
The ship without the wave of force
The sky without the clouds
Feel restless and remain pity
You are that small factor for me

*

No talks between us for a day
Makes me feel alone
Whilst the sun kisses the river at set
Among the ray, I remain
To see you at least in a day

*

My friends probably feel
Lucky enough to have me with them
What about my luck?
Which lies in you and your love
Grateful to have you as my Luck

*

It is only you whom I think
When I write and sing
This happens only to me?
I do not care about that
Just live and be with me.

*

That one person who gives us kicks to rise daily and come see them just for our breaths to be taken away. We are crushed so hard, especially for the first few times that the person almost becomes addicted to us. We wait for them the whole day just to catch a glimpse of them.

"Things we do in love are absurdly silly"

42. Lost everything

God exists or not
Maybe a unjust matter
But one who raises you up
From an infant to a human who's better

*

He sat aside the grave
Laid one after another
He wept a lot in mourn
As he sat on the stone further

*

The first grave was his mothers
He remembers her smiling face
Her care for him and others
Made him memorize with a sad face

*

The punishments felt cold-blooded
Did not know you were doing good
Just you stayed down every time
To hold me with your motherhood

*

I lie today helpless beside
Missing your talks laugh
Those ill happening with me

Which you cover and sort
*

As he thought of her
He also knew the other God
Which made him move up
To another grave of his father, oh lord!
*

You said once
That you will never leave me alone
At last, you betrayed your promise
He said with a gaping tone
*

One who cradled, held my hand
When I walk ready to catch
Left me with the forbidden thing
I want you... He had a gasp
*

With words boggling his throat
Somehow, he tried to say
I want your cheers for my grace
And want to laugh and play
*

The world seems untruth
He cursed himself
He is left with nothing, he knew
But with two Graves with 'less help'
*

As he stood to retreat
Someone held his hand
"Mother..." He started to sob
But soon the hand slipped off like the sand
*

I wanted you I am only 12
Should I yell at you?
So that you can come back
And tell me I love you!
*

Dad used to say hold the hand
Help others to seek one
I failed to save you
And in return, I got to mourn
*

I just wanted to say one thing
As he turned around
I will remember my betrayal
And you will be found
*

The sweet memories
Clashed upon one another
His cheeks red as his eyes
But that he would not bother.
*

I am extremely fortunate to receive that love and continue
receiving the same in the future for a very long time

(TOUCHWOOD).

There is that intense feeling that clenches your heart and stomach that they are getting old in front of you and it is the law of nature that you cannot stop.

I can only imagine what someone feels if that happens at a very young age or at any age for that matter.

Just go give them hugs and kisses it should not be coming from me rather you would have done it yesterday and continue tomorrow.

Share your days with them because that is the only thing this poor mind cherishes.

43. Bizarre

The situation is worse, tensed
None to come, none to go
Vulnerable the opportunities are
Do not know, what I know

*

About him, I read his face
With a glimpse of a smile, he looked
Kept all his feelings in his inner self
Exam and me as if I am crooked

*

As nature gives both life and death
We too had two rough roads
One with writing and writing
And others with exams on boards

*

We stand against a diverged road
Which can change the future
The one not taken will surely
Haunt us hereafter

*

The plans seem easy
Easy only we think of it
Practical in the society

It creates slow to a big hit
*

We live here with truth aside
Taking along the pressure
Not of our wish it is put
It is to make our 'bright future'
*

The so-called 'civilized society'
Should know what it really needs
Not one which the other say
It should not put its greed
*

I with my acquaintances
Will be what we want
Whether we get accepted or not
We will ignore their harassing taunts
*

Look for the talent in you
Not for the option which all have taken
Make a unique way of yours
One which cannot be bent or beaten
*

I still look at his face
With a glimpse of a smile in return
And I think for the better
One Road to take, a life-changing turn.
*

Examinations surely take a toll on us, especially me. It was one such exam of many that I do not remember or could care less for that made me question my choice. Well for me really it was not much a choice but nonetheless, **I am to blame here isn't it?**

And maybe it is not only about exams but also every part of our lives that hits a dead end. We know there are many ways to go but we also must not forget that they are not options just an illusion of free will!

I did not take the road that was less travelled but I do explore that realm a tiny bit here and there through things I write.

Will I ever walk on that path completely? Probably not.

44. When you turned and smiled

The situation tensed, heated up
All boiling in the hatred's sin
Sparkling and delightful is your stance
With your face smiling

*

The world could be stopped
For spectating your love-side
I am just a human
And have a heart hidden inside

*

Involuntary is its action
But pounds and cowers seeing you
Not in fear, actually yes!
It is afraid to fall in love with you

*

You turned and smiled
Were you seeing me?
Yes! I know it was a lie
A lie? Let it be

*

A sweet moment passed
And passed in a second

My blank face read your smile
And those lips are soon vacant
*

I cogitated about that moment again
Stood still and thought more
Was I the only lucky one?
Or else one among sea shells on the seashore
*

I tried to respond
With an awkward glimpse of a smile
Those lips never liked it
But this time went apart for a mile
*

The lie turned into the truth
The truth of love and faith
It was not me, but others
'Love! It is already very late.'
*

Smiled sheepishly as I wrote this. We all remember that moment, that one moment when we realized we do have butterflies in our stomachs. We really thought that this world could be beautiful if you saw the person you have fallen in love with, daily. But soon that fades because innocence cannot be hidden under the truth of reality. Not being optimistic right? I know.
But what if those butterflies were beautiful and full of colors?

45. Classroom talkies

The swag runs along
All the way through
Making a bond with others
Who likes swag and you.

*

Gangs are made often
And a weird name is kept
After a controversy
Rarely they wept

*

The classroom also has fun
And surely some love birds
Securing a place for them
Away from other muds

*

They refuse they love
But sometimes agree
The love waits for them
If they do not betray and flee

*

The talkies do not end here
Some secrets become knots
Relationship and friendship break

The heart with ego, clots!
*

When it comes to unity
All are one again
Glaring at the enemy
And get peace, without pain
*

The shade of teachers,
Make it 'better cool'
Teachers also are bitter
Innocents make them fool
*

"The classroom talkies"
Are very famous among all
If one does not exist in class
It creates a deep downfall
*

One needs to experience it
The love and hate
It touches our heart
The classroom talkies await!
*

The school can be awesome and loving if you get into the
right kind of people. I know you will be thinking how can
someone judge what the tender mind thinks at that age. But
trust me when I say this,

"You carry most of your emotional traumas and baggage from your schools,"

You form opinions and rarely if you are clever enough will understand how this world works. There is a wickedness in each of us that is present hiding behind the innocence of age.

46. The Wolf and the Moon

The moon has spots
Maybe because of someone's betrayal
But still, it enjoys his company
Making its face gleam and being loyal

*

The anguished cry of wolf
Makes us annoying
The wolf cogitates about the moon
And cries aloud, worrying.

*

'Oh! Lord let me reach her
She awaits, she will turn black'
The gurgling sound of cloud
Made him to step back

*

'He abandoned me
Living me a cold death
Didn't he leave me?
Asked underneath a sad breath

*

The sun sets in vain
Saddened birds cry aloud

They will not care for others' love
Rather they argue and shout
*

Cursing the Lone-wolf
Growing wilder than ever
But had a little space
For a 'love-forever'
*

Loving the moon
Was never easy
I cried at nights
He could not reach there, but see.
*

The moon and the wolf are symbols of lovers who never achieve what they long for. They find themselves in that incomplete relationship.

As they say 'If it is true, it will surely be hard to get.'

47. Sorry

Caring for a person
You surely do it
A person you love
Will be a good-luck hit
*

Only not just caring
Also respecting them
No offense is done
Happiness overwhelms
*

A friend like you
Counts a lot to me
You are like 'Laurel'
A vast thoughtful sea
*

A slipshod, I am
I ignored you, sorely
'Sorry' could not change
The memory, a ghastly
*

Today sitting alone
Felt your absence
The nature gurgling words

Informing your presence

*

The time we spent
Where sweetest of all
Memories will not follow
Though I would be old and fall

*

Sorry again, for everything
Ignoring mainly, I know
May you understand
What I wanted to convey and show.

*

Times like these are tough. They are tough on your ego and self-respect. These are the times that allow us to strengthen the bonds. Friendship does not care about the sorry but our subconscious does. It may seem like just a word to you and me but the mountain of burden it carries or the flood that it is holding is not that easy to understand.

"Sorry doesn't solve anything when you do not allow yourself to heal"

48. Decide

You do not have time
Said an intellectual man
Decide your future now
Ordered with the same tan

*

He was my father
Sitting on a chair
Held his hand in vain
Deciding my life to be fair

*

I swallowed it in pain
'Decide or else...,' said I
The future was at stake
Time is for truth not lie

*

I want to choose an aim
Which follows my father
And should cope up
With my dreams rather.

*

Confused I am
Swallowing a decision
Though I wanted to take one

But skipped with precision
*

Abundance of choices
I have, one to choose
A lifetime decision
Or else I would lose
*

A smiled escape
Changing the mood
And made my day
Which actually should
*

The decision is pending
It has a long wait
'Pick the decision now,
Or it will be too late.'
*

We all have crossed paths like these at least a few times in our
lives.

Did we care?

In the end, everything comes to life in the same manner as it
is written. Everything ends well eventually and when you
look back the decisions you took seem right and that is why
you ended up here.

Does free will really exist or do we just forget what decisions
led us here?

49. The Writer's song

"Write, Written, Wrote"
This is the first line of the song
Nothing better than this, could replace
As they are, for which writers long

*

'Deep and Intense' the story should be
Say his mini version within.
He hears him with ears open
And writes with a thoughtful sin

*

Twist and turns are part of the climax
The story must go on
Making a drift, imagine new
With some action of ding dong

*

Comedy and humor must be real
It is better to bring it up
Now that you can make one laugh
Your song gets a level-up

*

If someone dies how pitiful it is
The emotions give you a boost
The little writer writes up hard

With people in funeral's pursuit
*

Turn back with a flashback
Memories clench the song's grip
Thoughts are changed one way or other
Turning in a future trip
*

No one cares if it is bad
Who will listen to you?
How will they react to it?
You love it, that is a must. Do you?
*

Completed it finally
Done with your work and skill
It is not the end but the start
Write till your heart is full
*

"The writer's song, is not his life"
It is his journey to goal
It is not only his, but everyone's
It is their combined 'Heart and Soul.'
*

For a writer, every piece written is out of the box because it comes from the depths of the mind which are left unexplored. There is always a reader's take on the piece. There is always a discrepancy because the reader's mind is itself unique and sometimes the readers merely understand the depth of poetry.

It is not poetry till you find the meaning of the words and lines. Also, things that are hidden in plain sight.

"Meanings in disguise is the essence of poetry"

50. Taken aback

The Merry rings of the bell
Mark your presence around
Turning towards the yellow wood
I hear your foot sound
Do you still remember our brotherhood?

*

Be calm, stay away, I will return
Burning fire, even the ashes
The wind blows outward and in turn
Slowing like deadly poison
Among me, under which love burns

*

Looking at these crunches in leaves
Waving a hand at you
The rain of memories cleaves
Spring of Forest grew
Memories haunt me, will you too?

*

Far away from a childish canopy
The blind eye searches for you
Hoping to pass a little glow
Tears trickle down only a few
They travel down deep within they slyly flow

*

Inside the dreams of you within
Goes all the way apparent
With the voice of silence
Rose the thought of the song
A beautiful truth followed by the intense

*

I will be taken aback
By the words, I would hear
By the face, I would see
By the heart, I would be judged
I will withstand and not flee

*

A pale light in intense dark
Appeared, clearing the mist
It was you, I hope
At last, under dim starlight
It is not him others insist.

*

A wild fantasy tale perhaps…

51. A Lonely birthday

Weeks away ahead
Is the "name day"
Well wishers know the occasion
And others scarcely say "Happy birthday"
*

The news made me
Horror struck with a downfall
Helped them to erase
The 'special' in that day's call
*

Sun sets today and he leaves
And returns after a holiday
The day just passes on
I do not have anything to say
*

He travels alone leaving me
With his small memories of the past
'That birthday was a blast'
And that is the thing to say at last
*

Blessed me with good health
Making me obese by his love
Today it hurts a lot

In his absence, the motionless move

*

I wish he fulfills the need
May his good deeds overcome
And turn out the things
Leaving me silly stories only some

*

He would also turn us
In the same month, I was born
I will not make him hopeless
Also being with him on the path of thorn

*

Tiresome and recklessly
I do not know how to write and speak
Tears in my eyes
And I know I will spend a "lonely birthday"

*

HE here refers to my father who was away for my birthday and my innocence was so underwhelmed by that news that I could not contain myself.

What is "special" without the people you love the most being around you on your special day?

Well, the birthdays do not matter to me as much as they did before maybe I am just turning out to be like my dad.

Finally!

52. Two Ways

The world seems to be at a halt
The conscience at stake
I sat with my pet
Beside the green lake
*

The pet slurped the water
Scarcely putting it in the mouth
Scratched behind his ears
With a small pity pout
*

Thoughts gargled the fluids
The brain seemed to tickle
I grasped my pants in my palms
Provided a little wrinkle
*

The lake took turns
And the life awaits of turns
The animal feared dark
Behind me, the dark "floods"
*

It was my past
The dog's eyes gleamed
When I saw ahead

With a frown, I leaned

*

It was the future, bright and blur
Something waits for me
Ahead I have a life
The dog also could see

*

All things faded slowly
The dog barked at me
It is now evening
And the brightness to flee

*

I stood, wiped my forehead
The sweat I cleared in the water
And forced my thought aback
Rain fell heavily, and I went for shelter.

*

You may feel most of the things are not clear because we are either living in the past or the future. We do not want to get out of that. We feel safe here. The past is the things we have accepted, and care less about what really the future holds for us.

Too stubborn to let go of the past or too ignorant of what the future holds?

SHELTER in the last line is the "present" we are living in.

53. All Along

Water reflects your image
But only the tears know
Who you are...
Only your eyes bear the pain
Bears the heartbroken.

*

Being an introvert
You cry when it rains
You need the rain to fall forever
It stops every time
Leaving you alone
Same old empty-hearted.

*

Dawn is the time when you are out
Sitting alone amid the world's rise
The sun rises over
It touches you as once she did
Your tears roll out
You gently clench your fist feeling the warmth.

*

Walking barefoot on the grass
It tickles your feet as she did
With her hair tangled to your foot

The smile on her face
Made you laugh bearing the pain.

*

You know she is leaving you
Because someone loves her
More than you, more than anyone would
Still smiling all along.

*

Gentle Breeze tells you her stories
You never knew where it comes from
From your heart or from hers
Ears turn to stories
And closed eyes make you feel her.

*

It was the last time we sat here
On the same bench
They know every bit of her and me.

*

Now I talk to them when she is gone
Someone loved her more than me
We talk all day long.

*

We are always afraid of losing someone. Someone or something. It does not matter because what really matters is the loss of feelings that are attached to that certain person or thing. We hold it too tightly and sometimes just crush the whole thing or even the person. But that loss teaches us many things. Things that are only learned through the pain.

Is it the person?

Is it the thing?

Or

Is it the feelings?

54. The Books Do Talk

The wind blew through the window
Playing with my hair, a little
Putting it over my eye
I could not get my hair off
Just felt helpless for a moment
Seeing my legs dead
And my hopes too.

*

Then I sniffed something usual
The Biblichor, the smell of old books
Which I had collected since my childhood
Now they talk to me
When I sit alone on my rocking chair.

*

There were lots of them
Everyone had a story to tell
About their hero who never lost
About the person, strong by heart.

*

Winners never quit
And quitters never win
I have heard it in many
When you work hard

You get all the gold in the end.
*

The books are covered in dust
They were all fantasies
Which took me higher
Took me to the world
Which I had never imagined.
*

I remember the king
Who fought fearlessly for his throne
And I can still recall the dialogue
"In the Game of Thrones, you win or you die there is no
middle ground."
*

I sit on my throne
But no one to take it away
And no one could too.
*

They speak when I am feeling alone
And I do not feel alone
When they speak to me.
*

I never liked reading books, never. But the lines took me to
somewhere where I did not belong. They took me to their
world and I could really see myself as the third person in the
stories. The time passed by so soon when I was in their world
breathing their air. Smiling, shocked, sad, every feeling I

would translate from those lines.

Ever thought, whether the book needs us or we need the books?

55. This World Is Not for Me

Though you get loved by all
All the care and the support
No one will need you after them
Just in their thoughts, you stay
Not by all, but only by a few men.

*

The world is quite small for me
I have wings but cannot fly
I am caged by the bounds of society
No one cares when it comes to them
You die down in that cage guilty.

*

Have you heard of Genius?
Does the norm thread hold too long?
They are working spirit and an idea
Makes the world to long for them
And for ages, they sing their songs.

*

Unique ideas are always different
The work is also amusing
But being "different" is it bad?
Remember life gives you one chance

I followed it and I grabbed.
*

Norms and rules are made by men
Could be amended with their demands
Could be rejected after you
Was it made to hinder you or stultify?
Or a way to successful plans?
*

Raise the bar of your work
Get up and be above your limits
No one will touch you if you raise high
Tomorrow comes every day
The times today never return.
*

How am I different?
The question everyone asks
But only some find the law
The law that makes the genius
The law comes at no intuition flaw.
*

Everyone is born with it
Do not ever compare yourself to them
They have their laws their time
You should not get frustrated matching it
Your time is in you and in none of them.
*

Sounds you may hear

A lot of different voices
All spitting at you at once
Some blocking the path you take
Clear your mind take up your choice.

*

Parents compare you with them
The whole world does the same
Let them get insane, not you
Dreams you see, work you do
From there it is not always the same.

*

This thing fires me up even today. I do not know what triggered me to write this but it's true. It is like a mirror in front of you, it shows how special you are and what you can become.

Always there will be someone whom you will be compared with but that does not make you less unique than them. What if, you have conquered that thought and worked on it. **Do you think you will want success in the end or peace with yourself?**

56. Before you

Before you,
The leaves chattered
The birds chirped
The air blew
Telling me their tales
Which they bore from miles
Tales of love and hate
Tale of reversal of fate.

*

Before you,
I listened to them
And did not ever speak
The words were "a boon"
They wiped my tears off
They helped me to understand
The truth that I could not withstand.

*

Before you,
I was not evil
I was not good either
But my soul did not hurt anyone
Except for its own self
Today it hurts for others

By the betrayals I have done.

*

There is a shift in our worlds when we meet a person of interest.

Their habits become ours, their things become ours, and their everything becomes ours. We certainly put value and our feelings out for that person.

There is one thing to understand they are just ordinary people, with your love, with your expectations, with your efforts make them special, make them what they are to you.

It is an illusion.

"Is that person special? Or do we make them special?"

57. The Hunger Strike

The watch at lanes
Goes my sight to them
The skin ones are out
With the clothing insane

*

Bones trap them from sides
The "in growths" shows in
Poverty they hide
From their poor older sin

*

Hunger strikes deep within
From all the gazes upon
I shall die here with it
And my children bear the hunger on

*

They shall help us
When they think the time has come
They shall borrow our hunger
And save us from slum

*

My son would be a cleaner
My daughter is a maid
I would die of a disease

Can our hunger ever fade?

*

A rich man I am
That at least my wife's dead
She would also have been rich
As she died without a tear shed

*

Someday the world will change
I would see from up there
The hunger strike ends
And all will live with love and care.

*

Ahem! I might not have really thought this through but the tender mind of mine grasped this early on. As of today, I may not have the same views or maybe too ignorant? I do not know.

58. The Post Stories

There are people
With many stories
All of them alike
Apart from their glories
*

My stories are simple
Most of it you have known
Before you I was unheard
After you I became unknown
*

Shadows do not lie
About the heart and the soul
Without you, incomplete
With you, I was whole
*

The world's happiness and cries
Does not matter to me
It is you, all I have known
Beside you, I cannot see
*

What truly matters is
You and me, not the world
Mistakes have been made

Without uttering a word

*

Even the wingless birds
Fly in my dreams
But I do have wings to fly
Cannot I fly to make their dreams true?

*

Deep in me, inside the dark
Their lives someone who knows
The future is not worth "the present"
It is a present but for who?

*

You may think of one
Who will be with you for life
Are there not others?
Who did really care for you?

*

The world is a big thing
To deal with it at once
When, where, what happens
No one so sure can know

*

The less people you meet
The better you get treated
At last, who knows the birds
Which whispers or flies for you?

*

Dreams of me are not big
Though they can contain the sun
Inside me the dark lives
For whom I will fly, cannot say for sure.

*

There is, no thought behind this one or is there something hiding so fine in between these lines like the fine print. Important, yet ignored. So, it is up to you, what do you think about your "POST STORY"?

Can you make your Dreams fly?

59. From One to Another

From one eye, you see the light
From others, you see the dark
What is the difference?
In the man's sweet lie
And in the dog's restless bark

*

From one eye you see good
From another, the bad
What is the difference?
In the sinful happiness
And in blissfully sad

*

All the white lies in you
And even the black
Sell your white in barter
Take the wiseness back.

*

There is nothing white and white. It's all gray. The meaning is that you always get the two sides of a thing. Of everything. There is always another side and you know it. You just ignore it.

YOU CHOOSE TO IGNORE IT. Because who does not want to be right, right?

60. An Old Man's Hope

The creaking chair's sound
Filled his emptiness and vanity
To and fro the old man goes
Day or night does not matter.

*

Having said that, he is an old man
He has a family too
Not big enough, for his depression
Neither to hold his trembling hands

*

He has fear of nothing
Even death gave up on him
He said watching the sun set and rise
Sometimes gazes over his books

*

When the light falls in
He sees the most beautiful thing
Encased in a small frame
His lips escape a smile and tears roll

*

Though all the emptiness he has
His hope fills his life and room
Thinking of only one

Waiting for his son to return
*

Every day the clock ticks
Forgetting all, but his hope
That his son will return, for sure
To not cry is his trick
*

One day the sun will rise
His son will come to him
But will look like **"in disguise"**
Only his palm on his shoulder will do
*

Did he know it was today?
Son returned after years
He felt the warmth
Maybe for the last time
*

Head turned and eyes met
One cried, and the other laughed
Only eyes spoke that day
Even the hearts were able to hear
*

Trembling hands had a support
Cleared vision of his,
Saw a stocky man
Whom the word calls a 'soldier'
*

It was, where the rainbow met Earth
It is when the long wait ends
Old eyes saw heaven in home
Ever thought of being alone?

*

He lived happily ever after
But only in his son's dream
Still the chair creaks
The old man sits there daily.

*

Can you get the meaning that, the sun, that was there the whole time did not give him the warmth that he needed. It was only when his son returned, he finally felt it.
Isn't that special for every father?

61. Walking beside the sea

I was walking beside the sea
It was my future, I foresee
My footprints vanished just like that
And on a branch, there was a bat

*

Before my visions were clear
It all turned on, my fear,,,,,,,,,,,,,,,,
Ran all along the coast
And saw that all my paths were closed.

*

Hoping to be a bird
I started my day being absurd
Which can fly above the heads
Resting in the clouds' beds

*

But I was a fool to think so
Walking beside the sea, like a 'gringo'
Neither sea nor my foot had an end
I should walk or should I mend?

*

My past was gone without a twitch
And the future foreseen was in the ditch
But now I had only my present

It was time to be **omnipresent**.

*

I have seen many fortunes and fortune makers but I have not seen a person who knew he or she would make out of this and hit big. There is always something that holds back from inside, which is curious to explore, yet cannot become free to flow your thoughts everywhere to create chaos.

The sea shore is a metaphor for having a sea of opportunities in front of us yet we run only along the shore to be safe, not exploring what the depths of the ocean have for us.

62. Write for yourselves...